STRESS LESS COLORING:
PAISLEY PATTERNS

100+ COLORING PAGES FOR PEACE AND RELAXATION

Adams media
Avon, Massachusetts

Published by
Adams Media, a division of F+W Media, Inc.
57 Littlefield Street, Avon, MA 02322. U.S.A.
www.adamsmedia.com

Contains material adapted and abridged from *The Everything® Stress Management Book* by Eve Adamson, copyright © 2002 by F+W Media, Inc., ISBN 10: 1-58062-578-9, ISBN 13: 978-1-58062-578-4.

ISBN 10: 1-4405-8487-7
ISBN 13: 978-1-4405-8487-9

Printed in the United States of America.

20 19 18 17 16 15 14 13 12

Cover design by Sylvia McArdle.
Cover image © Olga Sadovnikova/123RF.

This book is available at quantity discounts for bulk purchases.
For information, please call 1-800-289-0963.

INTRODUCTION

Looking to relax? Want to feel more creative? Need more peace and quiet in your life?

If you're looking to get rid of all the extra stress in your life, just pick up a pencil, crayon, or marker and let *Stress Less Coloring: Paisley Patterns* help you manage your worries in a fun, easy, therapeutic way.

Over the years, studies have shown that coloring allows your mind to concentrate solely on the task at hand, which brings you into a restful state similar to what you can achieve through meditation. When you allow yourself to focus on the creative artwork in front of you, your mind doesn't have room for all the anxiety and stress in your life. And when your mind relaxes, your body follows by letting go of any tension and giving you a sense of peace and well-being.

Throughout the book, you'll find more than 100 black-and-white prints depicting a variety of swirling paisleys that are just waiting to be colored in. The beauty of these prints is that you can color them in however you'd like. The most relaxing colors are cool shades such as green, blue, and purple, but if you'd rather splash bold, bright hues like red, yellow, or orange across the page, feel free! Let your own unique palette guide your hand and personalize your pattern.

So whether you're new to art therapy or have been embracing the fun of coloring for years, it's time to stress less and find your inner calm and creativity—one paisley print at a time.

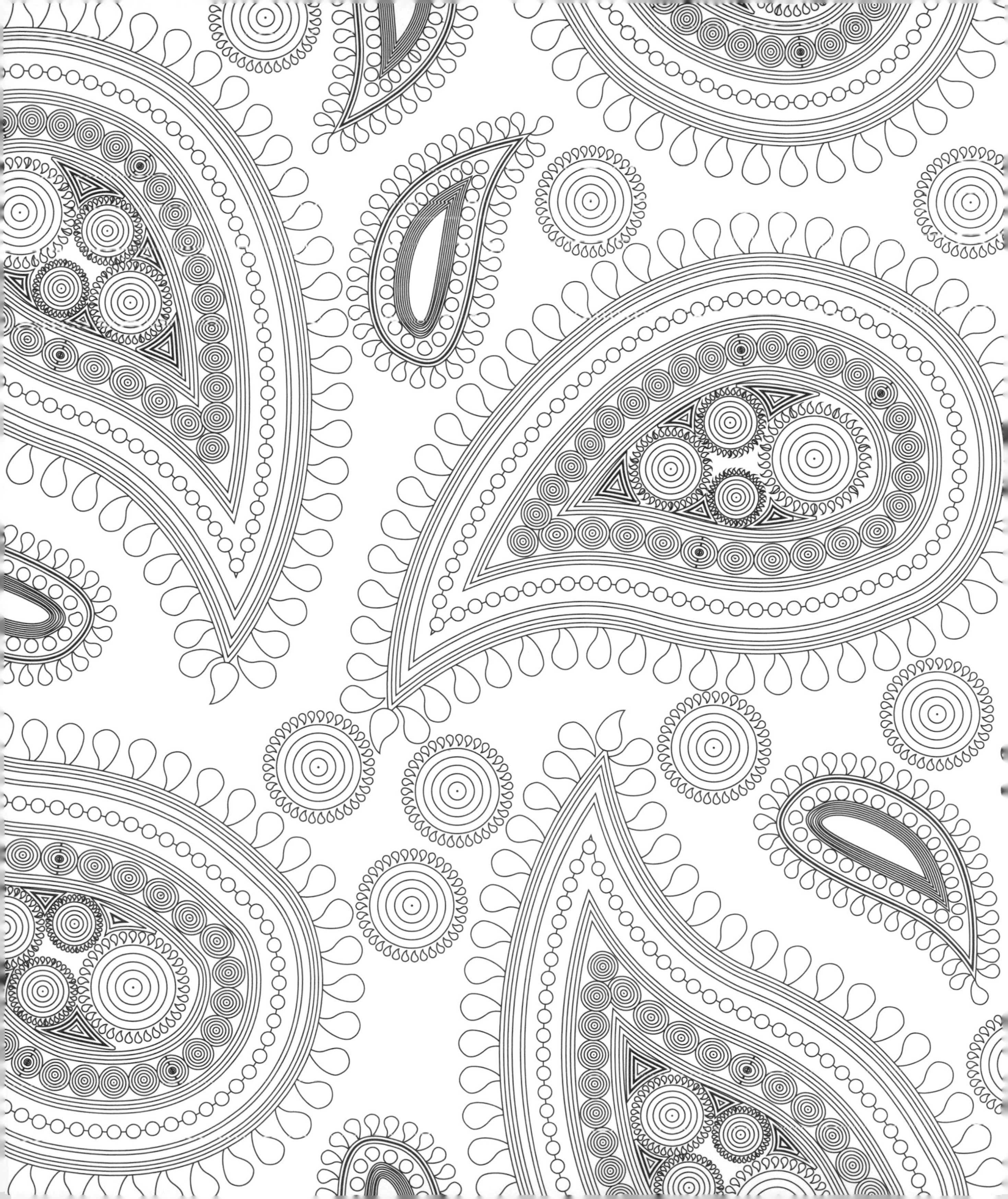

Image © iStockphoto.com/gfxwork

Image © iStockphoto.com/adroach

Image © iStockphoto.com/antoninaart

Image © irmairma/123RF

Image © iStockphoto.com/Attsetski

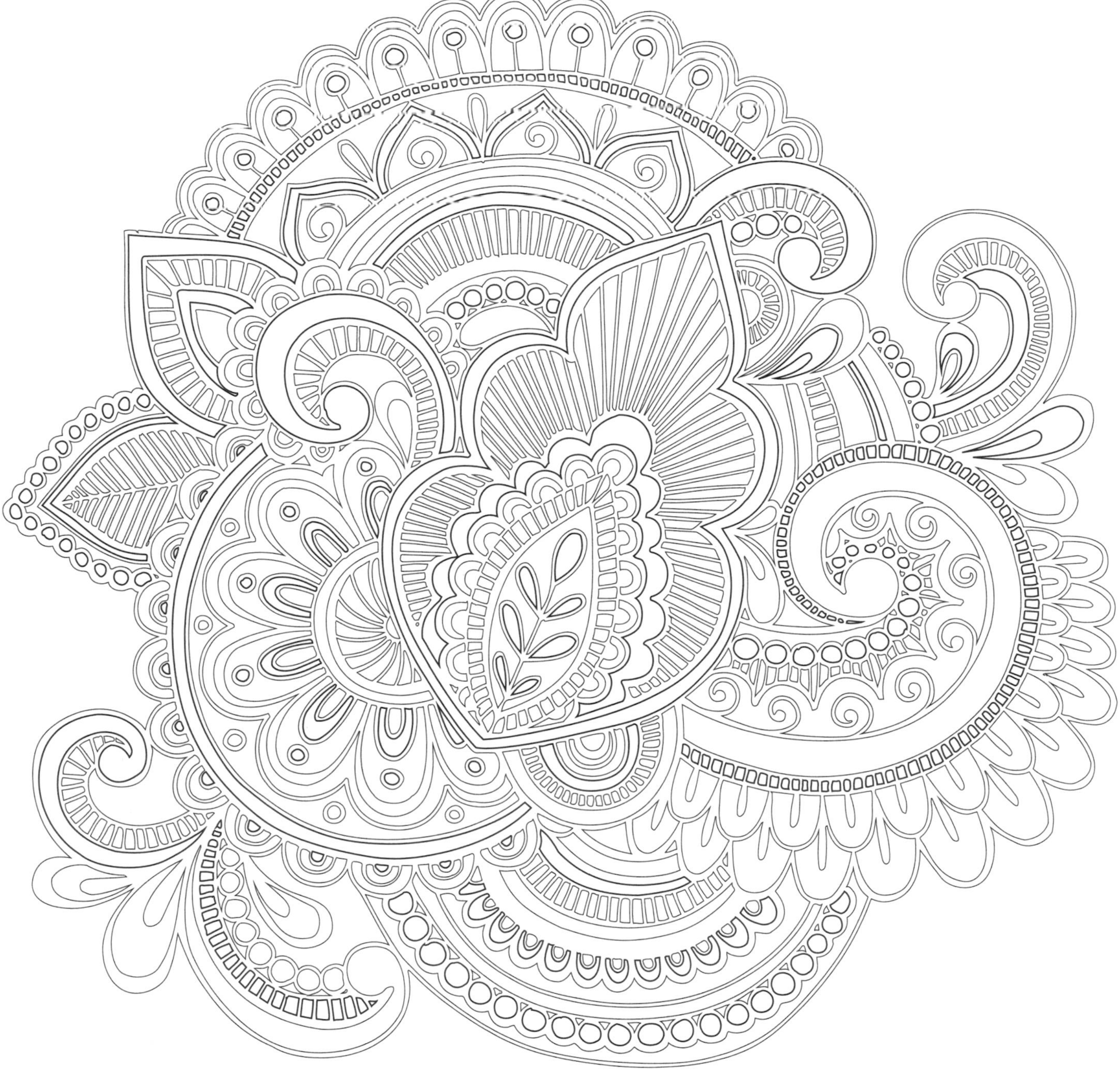

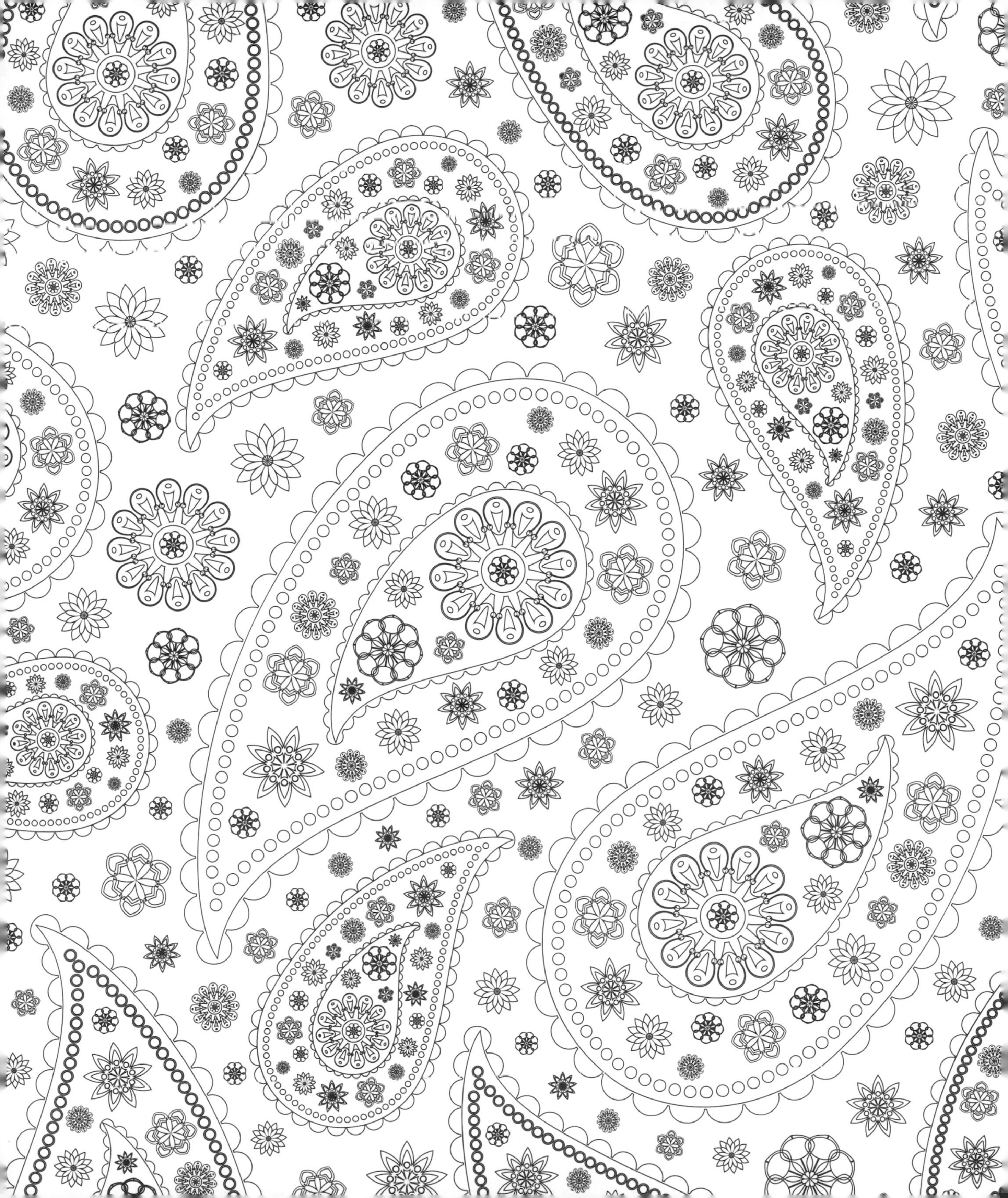

Image © iStockphoto.com/ratselmeister

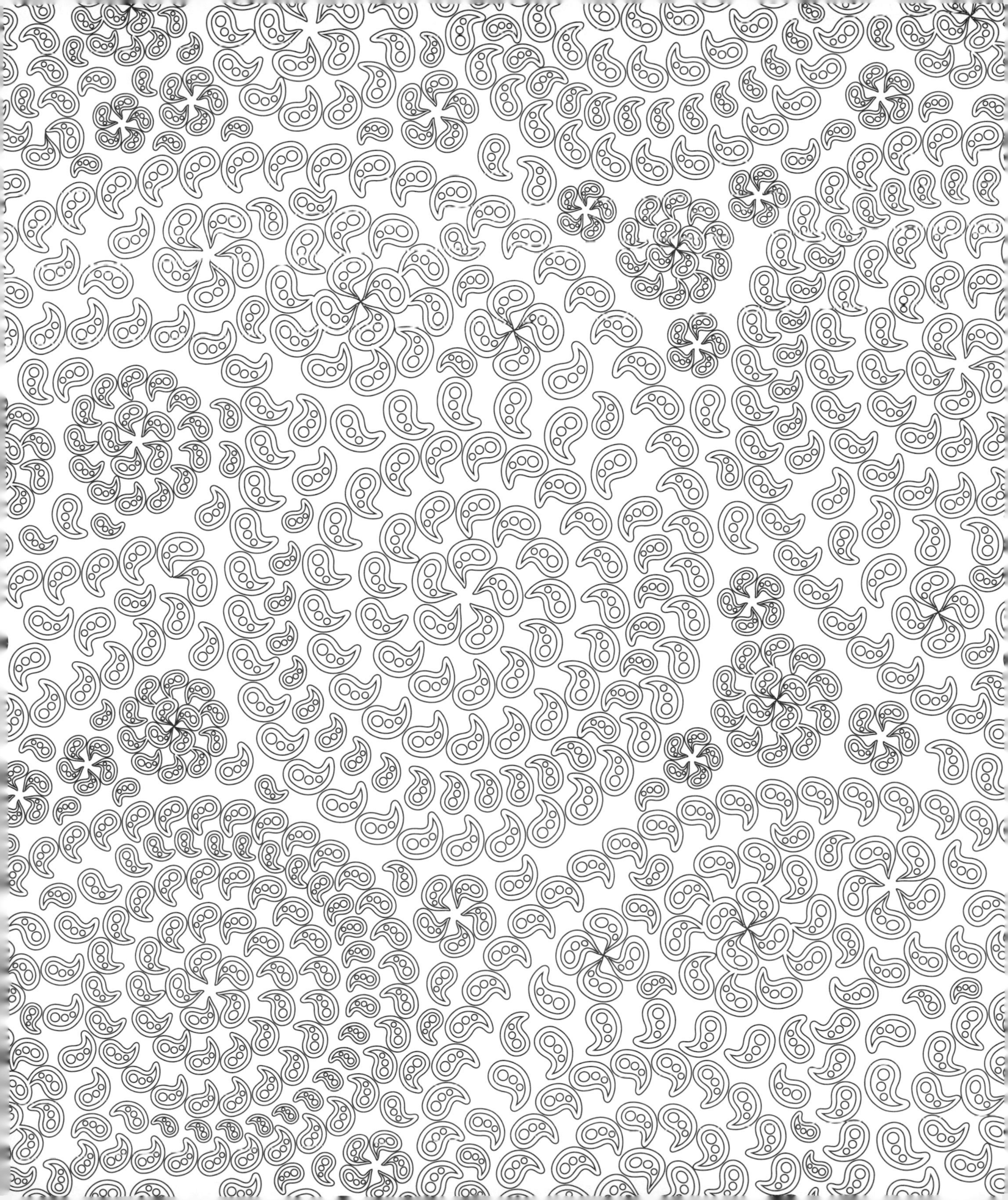

Image © iStockphoto.com/OlgaLIS

Image © Nilesh Malkani/123RF

Image © iStockphoto.com/il67

Image © iStockphoto.com/transiastock

Image © iStockphoto.com/AlfaOlga

Image © iStockphoto.com/melazerg